Broken Identity
OF THE
FATHER

CHAD WALLEN

ISBN 979-8-218-13960-5

Illustrated by Chad Boyd

Printed in the United States of America

About the Author:

My name is Chad Wallen and I'm 42 years old. I have a beautiful wife named Kelsey, three little girls, and a little foster baby. I have been a dad to sixteen kids, three being my own and thirteen I have had through co-parenting with the state. I was born, raised, and spent most of my adulthood in Oregon. I grew up playing soccer and baseball until about seventh grade where I shifted my focus to soccer. I played one outdoor and two indoor seasons per year. I enjoy many outdoor activities, but my favorite being fishing. The best ways I have found to relax after a stressful or heavy day at work are by working on cars, working on bikes, or cooking.

I accepted Jesus as a 15-year-old at a youth group event. I dug heavy into my relationship with Jesus until I was about 19 years old when I moved to Bend, Oregon, and lost my way. Nearly ten years and two cities later I was hit with quite a surprise, divorce. This pushed me into rekindling a relationship with Jesus.

About a year-and-a-half into my recovery, I was led to serve overseas in Thailand. During the process of the pre-trip meetings, trainings, and get togethers, I met my wife. God didn't just give me a wife, He gave me a gift. Our marriage has been laced with blessings, challenges, and God's provisions.

In 2018, we decided to sell the majority of our belongings, pack two small Uboxes, buy a motor home, fill it with the necessities, and head south with the intention to end up in Texas. This journey took us through six states in about five weeks. Our trip was cut a bit short with a broken engine in Granbury, Texas. Our home on wheels went to the shop for ten weeks with $5,900 worth of engine damage. Let's just say, after about a week, we were getting a little stir crazy in a hotel with three adults, three kids, and two dogs. We looked around for a place to live until we could find where we felt we were supposed to land. We are now living in Granbury, Texas, running a ministry for fatherless young men, raising our kids, and trying to do our part in the foster care world.

The Book...

Once upon a time…wait, we ain't gonna start that way. My life hasn't been a fairytale. It's had ups and downs but has had a clear pathway imprinted by the Lord.

Starting off, I was born in Salem, Oregon, and raised in Dallas, Oregon. Not "The Dalles" or Dallas, Texas, but Dallas, Oregon. My memories include my mom peeling out in front of our house in our 1985 Volkswagen Jetta, religiously going to mass at the Catholic Church, playing soccer, hooking my dad in the butt with a treble-hooked steelhead spinner while standing in the middle of a river, traveling to my grandparents' home in Washington, along with many other impactful things I will cover throughout these pages. Each of these events have had an impact on my life today.

We all go through thousands and even thousands of thousands of events throughout our life that adjust our thoughts, behaviors, and values, and reveal our calling. Throughout this book I will reveal stories from my past, current battles, and future goals. I will lead you through the path of how I got from the kid born and raised in Dallas, Oregon, to the 42-year-old man running a full-time ministry for fatherless young men.

Contents

Chapter 1

The End… at the Beginning.

After living 39 years in Oregon, moving around to different cities for my job and life changes, my wife and I were led to move to Texas. The last few years in Oregon were packed with the most obvious "spirit led" times in my life. It all started with reigniting my relationship with Jesus in 2010. I began serving in kids ministry at my church, was a facilitator in divorce care ministry, and participated in a mission trip to Thailand to work with kids who were rescued from being at risk of being sold into the sex trade.

Throughout it all, I had this clear overwhelming drive to mentor young men, specifically without a dad figure or positive male role model. At one point I was working on trying to start a non-profit that was specifically automotive based, working on one car at a time with three to four kids at a time. Unfortunately, I was quickly and directly discouraged because of the cost, logistics, and challenges of a non-profit.

Oddly enough, God opened a different door at a local single mom's ministry. I was approached about starting an activity for fatherless young men, but we weren't pigeonholed to automotive. We would be teaching things we felt like a dad would teach in the hopes of minimizing embarrassment when one of the attendees went back to school after the weekend. We wanted to come against the isolation when our attendees would hear from their peers, "My dad took me fishing this weekend" or "I worked on the car with my dad this weekend." The guys without dads would feel embarrassed because they never did those activities. They didn't have a dad to teach them those activities and didn't have the chance to experience them with their dad.

Seeing this need, Advance Camp was birthed with the goal of lessening the fatherless young men's embarrassment. I started out as the mentor coordinator with the intention to get men involved who had a heart for the fatherless and a drive to speak into young men's lives.

A few camps later I had another answer to prayer: I took over the activities, curriculum, and mentors. This was when Advance Camp really started to form into what it is today. After running camp for almost three years in Oregon, my wife and I decided to pursue the opportunity and the pull to move to Texas. This decision was preceded by prayer, fasting, seeking wisdom from older mentors of mine, and waiting on the Lord. We experienced an abundance of guilt while considering moving to Texas. We knew we would be leaving behind our community, the foster care system, my Advance Camp young men, and the men's ministry that

I was very involved in. During our season of asking for guidance from the Lord, I had my mentors, pastoral leadership, and God speaking through sermons saying, "Have you thought about the fact that God has been training and developing you to plant Advance Camp in Texas?" I was finally at peace about the move knowing that we would be starting Advance Camp in Texas.

Our model here in Texas, and now spreading across the nation, is mentoring fatherless young men between sixth and twelfth grade while teaching them tangible skills we feel a father should have taught if he was still around; along with these skills, we teach the love of Christ.

"Which of you fathers, if your son asks for a fish, will give him a snake instead? Or if he asks for an egg, will give him a scorpion? If you then, though you are evil, know how to give good gifts to your children, how much more will your Father in heaven give the Holy Spirit to those who ask him!"

Luke 11:11-14 (NIV)

Chapter 2

My Dad...

My dad was the product of the baby boomer generation where men worked their tails off, provided for their family almost to a fault, and knew how to work with their hands. Their words and commitments meant something, but this generation of men also didn't say "I love you," give hugs, or verbalize they were proud of you. Of course, there are the one-offs who don't fit this description, but they were the exception. Even though these men never verbalized it, they too sought love, respect, and validation. They typically didn't receive it, and weren't allowed to express it, so they couldn't pass it on with ease. This generational behavior was passed on by my grandfather to my dad, and ultimately to me. When you grow up in an environment where the kids are supposed to be seen and not heard, relationships between a father and son are not encouraged or supported. Yet these relationships are instrumental to a young man growing up, especially with validation. Besides the need for validation, every young man needs to feel loved by his father or a positive male role model to develop into a strong, distinguished, and respectful man. He can't be taught how to become a man from his mom or auntie. While women have powerful roles in a young man's life, how to become a man is not one of them.

I can still remember traveling from Dallas, Oregon, to Lynwood, Washington, to visit my grandparents, my dad's mom and dad. Organizing the landmarks in my head as we passed them driving up I5 I felt like I could already smell my grandma's perfume and the smell of beer and cigarettes on my grandpa as we were pulling into Lynwood. As we got to their house, we were always met by my grandmother while my grandfather was in the living room watching whatever sporting event happened to be on. He would say a typical "Hello" to the family, occasionally hug us grandkids, but just a hello, smile, and head nod to my dad. My grandparents seemed to coexist really well, not show much PDA, and keep public communication to a minimum. This all fed into the reality of a lack of "words of affirmation" and the positive example to the next generation.

As we would get settled with our visit, Grandpa would sit in his Lazyboy, beer on his old wood end table and magazine rack, pack of cigarettes in his shirt pocket, and locked into the golf channel. As my grandfather sat in his chair, I watched interactions between my dad and him. The topics would stay in a comfortable place of my dad's last hunting or fishing trip, weather, or some observation about a relative. The story wasn't much different when they visited our home; TV on, beer on the end table, and minimal conversation.

As I reflect back on these interactions, my dad never engaged with us during these times; we children were seen and not heard, and the father-son engagements were minimal across multiple generations. Can I hold my dad accountable for what was passed down to me? The lack of interaction and affection at greetings and goodbyes? Should I expect my dad to be different than what he had seen and learned? As a young child, that answer is absolutely yes. I remember aching for time with my dad and being acknowledged as one of the guys. I was searching for validation and seeking affirmation that I had value. My grandfather has since passed away, but my hellos and goodbyes still reflect my dad's interactions with his father, though my dad accepts my forced and awkward hugs. My intention is to break the generational behavior.

As I grew up, I remember my mom playing the majority of the parenting role, teaching role, and support role on a day-to-day basis. My dad, like earlier acknowledged, worked his tail off for our family. He put in 27 years at a lumber mill without complaining to us kids. He worked crazy hours, graveyard shifts, swing shifts, early mornings, and late nights. One thing I can NEVER say about my dad is that, he was lazy. I only remember short blips in my life with him watching "Nature" on OPB, or quietly reading the newspaper in the mornings. He was either working or engaging in his favorite outside activities of hunting and fishing.

Oh yeah, I promised to explain the story of the infamous "butt hook." My dad loved and loves to hunt and fish. There were many occasions my dad would take us as we got older and it was safer for us to join. As I remember the story, I was about 9 or 10 years old on the Siletz River steelhead fishing with my dad, my brother, my dad's best friend, and his son, who was also one of my friends. As I was standing in ankle deep water, watching my dad stand on a rock in the middle of the river that he had waded out to, I was thinking,

"How can I get my spinner far enough out to even have a chance of catching a fish." As I was standing next to my friend, we were joking back and forth that this would be a great time to learn how to "side arm cast." I flipped the bail arm, grabbing the line with my pointer finger, and feeling the cold-water drip down the line, I swung the rod back behind me. Once I completed the fully extended back swing, I launched the spinner back forward, releasing it with the hope of a productive landing. No splash happened. To this

day it still makes me chuckle a little bit. The look on my dad's face when that treble hook on the steelhead spinner sunk into his butt cheek, almost causing him to jump off the rock in shock. Let's just say my side arm cast needed some attention.

Until recently, my memories of my dad sharing his extra-curricular activities with us were heavily on the negative side. I'll go into more detail later about the shift. He would load us up in his truck, drive the gravel roads of Black Rock or Valsetz outside Fall City, Oregon, scouting for animals, shooting guns, shooting bows, hunting for mushrooms, and even finding some deep, hidden winter steelhead fishing holes.

Even with all that my dad did do with me, my brother, and my sister, wounds happened and validation was needed. I don't think my dad ever wounded us or skipped over the "love and validation" on purpose, but it happened. I've reflected back over this time and time again. Was I weak? Am I needy? Or was I just bluntly unaware of all I was being given.

13 Then Jesus came from Galilee to the Jordan to be baptized by John. 14 But John tried to deter him, saying, "I need to be baptized by you, and do you come to me?"

15 Jesus replied, "Let it be so now; it is proper for us to do this to fulfill all righteousness." Then John consented.

16 As soon as Jesus was baptized, he went up out of the water. At that moment heaven was opened, and he saw the Spirit of God descending like a dove and alighting on him. 17 And a voice from heaven said, "This is my Son, whom I love; with him I am well pleased." - Mathew 3:13-17 (NIV)

After reading about Jesus' baptism in the Jordan and the spirit descending on Him like a dove, and God specifically speaking over Him, I was given peace. If Jesus needed validation and love from his father, who am I to think I'm bigger, badder, or tougher to not need it. Thinking you are above Jesus is never a good place to be. I can still remember when it was, where I was, and even the weather outside when my dad told me for the first time that he loved me. I also remember the time, place, and reason why my dad told me he was proud of me. These two incidents were almost exactly 20 years apart. These were/are both very impactful moments in my life, as I am sure God speaking over Jesus was for Him as well.

"For the Spirit God gave us does not make us timid, but gives us power, love and self-discipline."

2 Timothy 1:7 (NIV)

Chapter 3

Am I the Man I'm Supposed to Be

"When he had finished speaking, he said to Simon, "Put out into deep water, and let down the nets for a catch." 5 Simon answered, "Master, we've worked hard all night and haven't caught anything. But because you say so, I will let down the nets." 6 When they had done so, they caught such a large number of fish that their nets began to break. 7 So they signaled their partners in the other boat to come and help them, and they came and filled both boats so full that they began to sink. 8 When Simon Peter saw this, he fell at Jesus' knees and said, "Go away from me, Lord; I am a sinful man!" 9 For he and all his companions were astonished at the catch of fish they had taken, 10 and so were James and John, the sons of Zebedee, Simon's partners. Then Jesus said to Simon, "Don't be afraid; from now on you will fish for people." 11 So they pulled their boats up on shore, left everything and followed him.

Luke 5:4-11 (NIV)

Am I humble, strong, and disciplined? What does this all mean? I continue to question myself about whether I am good enough to become the man I am supposed to be. This stems from two places: on the flesh side, a lack of validation from my dad, and on the spiritual side, I can never be. I'm not supposed to be good enough, strong enough, or smart enough on my own, but with God I am. Righteousness comes from God, strength comes from God, and wisdom comes from God. The more, I realize that, digest it, and accept it, the more I can move forward in a way to follow Christ better and fulfill His will in my life. I have noticed the times where I am more intentional with serving God daily I grow in my relationship and communion with Him, which makes me depend on Him more, reflect Him more, and become less like my environment-conditioned self.

To become the man God has made me to be, two intentions must be set. First, I must seek to become more like Jesus daily; and second, I must be intentional about fulfilling God's calling in my life.

The more time I spend with the Lord, the better I hear His voice and understand Him. I have gone through seasons of not hearing or feeling connected to the Lord at all and it is like walking down the old dirt street of a ghost town. There may be a purpose or was a purpose to this season, but all I see is tumble weeds and emptiness. When I stay in this place too long, I come to the conclusion that this is all my relationship with Jesus is supposed to be, dodging tumble weed and dusting your shoes, shuffling down a dirt street. The moment I look up, I realize that there are people in the buildings lining the dirt road, just waiting for someone to look past the facade, walk through the doors, and start a conversation. I see God as a father that says, "pull up a chair, pour a cup of coffee, and let's talk." This Father wants to teach me all He knows, sit beside me in a project, correct me when I am in the wrong so I can do better next time, wrap His arms around me and let me know I am loved and that He is proud of me.

I take "pray continually" literally. I am in constant communication with God. Sometimes our conversations are deep and wisdom gaining, sometimes I am advocating for others, sometimes it's just a light conversation of appreciation and love. For me, this is key; God loves us so much and He wants to spend as much time with us as we will let Him. Have you ever seen those two guys at work that spend so much time together that they have their own "language" of goofy sayings and sometimes voices that they make up? They only do it around each other at first, then it bleeds into the rest of their life. That's what I am seeking with God. Spending so much time with God gives Him opportunity after opportunity to speak His calling into my life.

I'm a bit of a slow learner. I prefer God to light up His will for me in Vegas Lights so there is NO WAY to misinterpret it. With my focus on God's success, not mine, but God's, I wait for blunt clarity to know where, what, and sometimes how I will accomplish His will for me. I so badly want to make sure I'm living life to the fullest in all God has for me, so I wait for Him, spend time with Him, and seek wisdom from Him.

As I am writing this book, I was approached to visit Nashville, Tennessee, to see about planting a camp location there. I had originally said no. God had never brought up Nashville in prayer or conversation. I had no heart ache for that state, and no doors had opened; just a buddy that said he sees a need. Side note, throw a dart at a map of the United States and you will hit a place that needs men to be fathers to the fatherless. I was in the midst of launching Oregon Camp and Florida Camp, so I truly felt God shut that down as an option for the time being. God's timing, not mine. Moving forward, a couple months after Florida kicked off, I felt, almost audibly, God say, "you can start the conversation." I took this as the opportunity to see what doors God had in the Nashville area. I reached out to my friend who was in the area and got the ball rolling, and what a ball it was. Doors started opening with a single mom's ministry wanting to partner with us, a pastor at a local church giving me the opportunity to share our mission and vision, and a retired pastor who wants to be involved who has knowledge, time, and a heart for the fatherless. Where this story was put on hold is when the yearly Texas snow storm and Tennessee ice storm rolled in the literal day I was supposed to travel. What do I do with this? It seemed like pretty clear opened doors, flashing Vegas lights, and the "God go ahead." I choose to rest in the fact that this is God's plan, but not God's timing. This is me understanding my role and God's plan, to become the man I am supposed to be, a man who seeks God and does His will. I rest in the place that God's plan is ALWAYS the best plan no matter how easy, hard, frustrating, or disappointing.

*"Yet to all who did receive
him, to those who believe in
His name, He gave the right to
become children of God."*

John 1:12 (NIV)

Chapter 4

Identity

As men, we generally believe that my father is who I will become. This isn't always bad but may just be "not good." My dad worked at a lumber mill, so will I work at a lumber mill. My dad is a drug dealer, so I will be a drug dealer. My dad is a murderer, so I will be a murderer. My dad is an abandoner, so I will be an abandoner. Our nature is to seek out our identity by any means necessary. The "dad identity" just happens to be the closet and most accessible to a young man seeking affirmation and love.

Have you ever done any foraging or hunting? The purpose or reason to do this is to gather and accumulate items to use later for another purpose. I relate the way we gather pieces of our identity to our sense of foraging. As we accumulate spoils from the foraging or hunting, we set them aside, storing them for later use, to fill in a gap or "need."

Starting out at a young age, we set out foraging or hunting for our identity. What naturally happens is we find pieces of that identity from our father, mother, friends, teachers, pastors, and the rest of the world around us. All these providers of identity impact us, but I have found none as strong of an impact as the father, especially for a young man. Along our life journey, we gather pieces of our identity and call on different pieces as they are needed.

Whether you want him to or not, your father impresses identities on you. The lie that is told to you is that you are or will become who your father is or was. Like I said, not always bad, but are we really living out OUR identity if we are living out our father's, or anyone else's for that matter?

We also naturally attach our father's behaviors to God's character. You say to yourself, "God will only be there when it's convenient because my earthly father was," or "I'm important to God and He loves me, but not as much as my neighbors." This is bondage that MUST be broken to truly embrace all God has for us.

I aim to live in a place of need versus want. Don't get me wrong, want sometimes beats out the need for sure. The world says you can be whatever you "want." This is misleading and dangerous. We come across many things in life that we want, but best-case scenario it's not fulfilling long term; worse case, it's destructive. The world says that I need notoriety, fame, money, the rush, and extravagant lifestyle to "keep up with the Joneses." I need to be important, have the house, own the trendy shoes, the fancy cars, and have the things that others look at me and say, "I want what he has". That is clearly a want that all ends and is forgotten at some point. None of these items are stored up in heaven. None of these wants can get you any closer to joy. None of these items can get you closer to your true identity that lasts. We aren't meant for these identities. We are meant for the identities that God gives us, the ones that really matter.

When you finally get to a place of breaking the bondage from your earthly father, break the bondage the world says about you, and embrace who God says you are, life gets better and clearer, not necessarily easier, just better.

1 Peter 2:9 (NIV)

"But you are a chosen people, a royal priesthood, a holy nation, God's special possession, that you may declare the praises of Him who called you out of the darkness into His wonderful life."

2 Corinthians 5:17 (NIV)

"Therefore, if anyone is in Christ, he is a new creation; old things have passed away; behold, all things have become new."

God says we are redeemed, we are adopted in as HIS children. We are chosen, we are called according to HIS purpose. We are no longer slaves to sin, we are created in HIS PERFECT image. We are prophets of the nations, chosen people, a royal priesthood, a Holy Nation, His special possession. We are no longer servants but a Friend of Jesus. We are conquerors, fearfully and wonderfully made. We are a new creation.

As I read through the identities that God gives me, and you, I can't help but think, do we allow ourselves to truly live out these identities? Do you make room for these identities? I encourage you to let go of your unhealthy identities given to you by an earthly source and replace them with the identities given to you by God. This is a daily and sometimes hourly practice of discipline. I have found that the closer I get to my identity in Christ, the closer I get to knowing my specific calling and living that out.

Chapter 5

The Fall Out

Imagine being a 12-year-old young man with a mom doing everything she can to create a loving, financially stable, supportive home, and all by herself. You watch your friends have a dad to come beside their mom as a partner, supporter, and provider. They have someone to throw a baseball with or talk about girls with. How often would you lie in bed at night and start a conversation with yourself saying "I wish"? I wish I had a dad to come to my game. I wish I had a dad to show me how to change the oil in the car. I wish my mom had someone to walk beside her. I wish I had a dad to fish with. The deep emptiness starts filling your head and flowing through the room. This is where the deep, deep damage starts.

When the emptiness is all encompassing and impacts behavior, it often continues into sadness, then commonly into anger. I don't believe that the majority of young men want to be angry, they just don't quite know what to do with the emptiness and the sadness.

Then there are the scars from the shrapnel – that's right, scars. Some of my least favorite words to hear from the young men I work with are, "I'm worthless," "I'm just a mistake," "I'm dumb," "I can't do anything right." These assumption and scars come from two main places: identities received, and identities self-assumed. I hear these phrases way too often by these young men. The positive side about them saying these things is that at least we know they are wanting to be smart, loved, appreciated, and affirmed.

The flip side of that is the guys who don't say anything and only allow those identities to build in their head. That inner dialogue is toxic to the wound they are trying heal and detrimental to becoming whole again. It makes it really difficult to assist with the healing process if the injury is hidden under layers of bandages and a false smile. I've watched a young man isolate himself, tell me he is bored, and not engage in a project because he is deeply damaged from a dad who rejected him and abandoned him, and the activity triggered all the scars inside of him. It took stepping away from the activity, engaging the young man, and choosing to be direct and real, before he opened up to dump out his hurt and scars. These are the "I have it all together" guys. I never let that facade deter me; it makes me be more intentional with listening and engaging them. Once these scars are created, they never go away but they are transformed. They transform into a story, a lesson, a reminder of an activity we prefer not to experience again. Sometimes it's a scar from a life-saving operation, an unfortunate tip over on a bike as you were learning to ride, the left behind reminder of a glass window that broke on your head instead of falling on your little sister, or maybe that time of rejection from a loved one, abandonment, silence when you really needed to hear words of affirmation, or that feeling of being left alone in the midst of "family."

Some of the scariest and deepest scars are what I call "the dad scars." These scars go deeper and last further into adulthood than most other scars received. Dad scars leave young men with a lack of what manhood looks like, and often abandonment issues. These are a gateway to pornography, addictions, and negative treatment of a lady. What the young men are left with is having a much higher chance of incarceration, homelessness, suicide, teen pregnancy, high school dropouts, and behavioral disorders. Currently the single biggest factor to a fallen society is the number of broken homes and consequentially fatherless homes.

The power of verbal love and validation to a boy or young man from his dad or positive male role model can change his trajectory. Remember, even Jesus received verbal love and validation from His father.

"He lifted me out of the slimy pit, out of the mud and mire; he set my feet on a rock and gave me a firm place to stand. He put a new song in my mouth, a hymn of praise to our God. Many will see and fear the LORD and put their trust in him."

Psalm 40:2-3 (NIV)

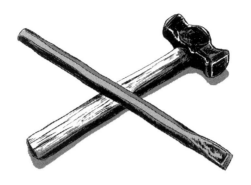

Chapter 6

Our Resolution

Pushing back against the world's agenda of a false identity is where we rest. Advance Camp stands in the gap that is left when a father isn't involved. Advance Camp exists to be an identity disrupter. I have taken my brokenness, my abandonment scars, my lack of affirmation and used it in a way to serve the single mom via mentoring the fatherless young men in order to break the cycle.

Advance Camp equips young men with tangible skills, with career-based trades, with words of affirmation, and it all comes with a side effect of confidence. When it comes to tangible skills and trade skills, I have found that young men, (or old for that matter,) have tunnel vision. "I only know what is right in front of my face." Tunnel vision breeds a lack of confidence, value, and hope.

I once heard a story of a young black man who wanted to work in the mill because his dad worked in a mill; he wanted to live in an apartment down the road and have a nice car, because that's what the people in his circle of influence did. He wanted all this because of tunnel vision. He only saw what was in front of him and what was expected of him. Until his dad told him, "Don't believe the lie." His dad told him and showed him he could have a different life. His dad's encouragement changed the trajectory of this young man's life.

The young men that come to Advance Camp learn a minimum of one new trade or tangible skill at every camp. We have had campers want to become electricians, plumbers, and even a farrier because we opened their peripheral vision outside the tunnel. Learning skills and trades have many layers of benefits. Two of the major benefits on the forefront are confidence and a lifelong usable skill. I once had a camper who refused to help his mom around their property doing "normal" property maintenance skills. The young man attended our lawn care camp where he ran a gas-powered weed eater, lawn mower, and a large chainsaw. The next day I received a photo from his mom with him starting the chainsaw she had tried to get him to start for years prior. This all happened due to a side-by-side taught skill. He went on to take care of many of the tasks his mom had requested all because he had built confidence within himself after tackling something he never had before.

I truly believe that young men go down paths of bad decisions because they haven't been given the ability, knowledge, and confidence to go down a path of quality productivity. Advance Camp is a place of prevention. It provides a productive path for these young men and the vast majority take it. A ministry leader who started a ministry to prevent children from being sold into the sex trade told me that if he finds the highest "at risk" group and gives them resources to no longer be at risk, he is 99.9% successful. Statistically if someone ended up in the sex trade and were recovered out of the trade, 40% would stay out while 60% would return because they knew no different. Advance Camp creates new paths for those at the highest risk of being incarcerated, homeless, suicidal, a high school dropout, or a teen parent. This makes them, statistically, less likely to go down these paths.

*"Pure religion and undefiled
before God and the Father is this,
To visit the fatherless and widows in
their affliction, and to keep himself
unspotted from the world."*

James 1:27 (NIV)

Chapter 7

The Call

When God called me to serve the "fatherless," He was very specific. The young men of Advance Camp are the backbone to the fatherless epidemic. As we help them to become better young men, better sons, better students, and better leaders, we will see the nuclear family gain strength, churches gain strength, communities gain strength, and the economy to make a shift for the better. When 75% of inmates are men from fatherless homes, 90% of homeless and runaways are from fatherless homes, and 71% of high school dropouts are from fatherless homes, how can the economy, community, and churches not grow stronger when we give them a valuable place to land. These young men are literally the axis point for the shift in our world.

We aren't all called to the same thing, clearly, but I do feel we are all called through the same voice, God's. We may hear it through prayer, scripture reading, an aching heart, a word from the Lord through someone, or through a dream, along with many others. I encourage you to meditate and pray over these questions below to start the conversation with God about your true calling.

God, how have you used me and prepared me? What have you, God, prepared me for? God, what do you want me to do with this preparation? God, who do you want me to serve? And, God, where do you want me to start?

Now is the time to start.

Step 1, Seek the Lord.

Step 2, Listen.

Step 3, Do.

I wrote this book with the intention to motivate, encourage, and give hope. I pray that anyone who picks up this book, reads it, and prays the prayer at the end becomes a world changer. I so strongly believe in you, that if you read my book and are moved by God to serve somehow, somewhere, I will take the time to pray with you and help guide you toward your mission. Reach me at my email: chad@advancecampusa.com.

PRAYER

PRAYER

Made in the USA
Columbia, SC
12 November 2024

45839093R00026